Cancer

Cancer

A Journey of Attitude and Gratitude

Terry Moore

CONTENTS

FAMILY AFFAIR

TEST AND PROCEDURES

SIDE EFFECTS

VICTORY

I want to dedicate this book to my brothers. My oldest brother Jack who lost his battle with cancer. My older brother Bob who is battling cancer and to my best friend Sharon who is a cancer survivor. I want to thank my good friend Kathy who always encourages me in all my endeavors. I also want to dedicate this book to everyone that has heard of someone, knows someone, or is someone that is dealing with cancer. I know firsthand how this disease can turn your world upside down.

Diagnosis

Story: Discovery of Lumps

∂

My brother came up to visit me one Sunday morning and he pointed out 2 lumps on the right side of his neck. They were small, around the size of a dime. When I felt them they were firm to the touch. I told him he should make an appointment to see his doctor.

Upon examination he was told that it was cysts and they would go away in a week or two and if they did not make another appointment. Well, they doubled their size within a 2 week period so he made another appointment. This time the doctor found another small lump behind my brother's left ear and another larger lump on the outer aspect of his left breast area. My brother was scheduled to have a consultation with a surgeon. After the consultation he was scheduled to have all the lumps removed the following day. Wow, things were moving at a fast pace.

The lumps were removed and sent to pathology and we were told we would get the pathology report in about a week. We returned to the surgeons office 10 days later to have the stitches removed and were told at that time that the specimens were sent out for more advanced studies. Neither one of us liked the sounds of that!

On July 27th we got the dreaded call from the surgeon, my brother has lymphoma, non-Hodgkin Follicular and B-cell cancer. Now we need to find a good oncologist.

To watch my brother cry was heart wrenching. He was scared and so was I. The stress level for both of us just hit 10 on a scale of 1 to 10 with 10 being the highest. I knew right then and there that I had to stop myself from walking down the dark side when thinking about this disease and what it could do. Things are going to get a bit challenging real soon. It's time to stay positive; it's time to be courageous, and help him do the same.

It's Cancer ©

By Terry Moore

It's Cancer – Oh no
Breathe in, let the energy flow

What will I do
Where to start I have no clue

I am scared, I am numb
I just want to hide, I just want to run

It's so overwhelming at first
Tears well up and I am ready to burst

It's OK to cry
It's OK to wonder why

It's an emotional roller coaster ride
I'll slow down and take it in stride

There is support and hope
It's there to help me cope

Asking questions is where I will begin
I will fight and I will win

Story: Stage 4 Cancer in Lymph and Bone

When my brother was told he had cancer in the lymph and bone he went pale and he cried. He was scared and so was I. We sat in silence for a while and then he got up and said I need to go home. I need to be alone. I under stood what was going on because I am the same way. He wanted to be alone to just take it all in and figure out what to do. His strength is found deep inside his core and that was where he was heading.

A couple of hours later he called me and said I am a fighter and I am not about to let this disease destroy me. I am scared. I am determined. I am ready to beat this thing.

I was just as scared for you see he is not just my brother he is my best friend. I made a promise right then that my brother would not go through this fight alone. I would be there for him.

Stage 4 Cancer ©

By Terry Moore

Stage 4 cancers in lymph and bone
I feel like I just entered the twilight zone

So many emotions running through my head
I just want to pull up the covers and hide in my bed

How long have I got
My stomach is all tied up in a knots

My first response was flight
My second response was fight

This diagnoses is larger than life
I have been a fighter all of my life

Do I lie down and just give up
Hell no, I am not about to just give up

My daily routine will be the same
Cancer my life you will not maim

There will be changes that's for sure
All for the reason to fight and to cure

Stage 4 cancers in lymph and bone
Cancer my plan is for you to be dethroned

Story: After 1st week

The first week after my brother's diagnosis of cancer there was a range of emotions that hit me hard. I experienced shock that goes along with the initial diagnosis, anger, confusion, fear, and an immense sense of commitment to be there for him. To make sure he would not be alone through any part of this disease process. My job is to help him stay positive and to learn to keep myself positive as well.

What I was not expecting was to learn what cancer is really all about and that I had some lessons to learn. Some lessons that surfaced was: it's about not having control, not knowing, having to have an endless supply of patience, giving, giving, giving, releasing, releasing, releasing, and so much more. Even through this horrific diagnosis I recognize that it also offered growth and development and how important it is to be receptive to new ways of thinking while traveling on this path that lies before us.

It's About ©

By Terry Moore

It's about not knowing
It's about saying
It's about believing
It's about praying

It's about asking
It's about releasing
It's about giving
It's about ceasing

It's about knowing
It's about faith
It's about flowing
It's about grace
It's about patience
It's about sharing
It's about love
It's about caring

Anger

Story: My Brother's Anger

My brother was angry. Angry that he had stopped smoking over 30 years ago. Angry that he had stopped drinking over 6 years ago. Angry that he had lost over 100 pounds. Angry that he had always ate nutritional food every day. Angry that he was walking 4 to 5 miles every day. He said, hell if I had known I was going to get cancer I would not have worked so hard to get healthy. What is the use because I got sick anyway?

I knew he was in the grieving process. We all know people out there that use and abuse their bodies and seem to be healthy as a horse. So I had to help him work through his angry. I mentioned that he was lucky that he had such a healthy life style because this was going to be a great benefit for him while going through the chemo treatments. I also said he was lucky because some get cancer then have to struggle to stop destructive behaviors to increase their chances of survival. I reminded him that he was lucky he had already made all the right choices many years ago.

I am so proud of my brother!

The Rules of the Game ©

By Terry Moore

Cancer you picked me today,
I did not choose to play.

The rules are not clear,
Is this to cause fear?

You play with my emotions,
What a notion.

You play with my eating,
My hunger is fleeting.

My GI you upset,
You want me to fret.

It's not happening, this game you play,
I am stronger than you, I'll be OK.

I will make the rules clear,
You will not cause fear.

Stay clear of my emotions,
That's my motion.

You can't control my eating,
Frequent meals prevent fleeting.

A bit of GI upset,

I refuse to fret.

It's not happening, this game that you play
I am a winner, so be on your way.

<u>Like it or not</u> ©

By Terry Moore

Cancer you don't make a sound
I know you are around

You're sneaky and cruel
You don't play by any rules

I will not be victimized
I will not be terrorized

I am taking a stand
I am fighting, understand

I am not a fool
I will do all that I can do

I will stay upbeat
I will not cower or retreat

I will give it my best shot
Like it or not

<u>Just go away</u> ©

By Terry Moore

Cancer you need to go away
Here you cannot stay

We do not want you in a lump
We do not want you in a bump

We do not like you in a male
We do not like you in a female

We do not want you here or there
We do not want you anywhere

One thing we know for sure
If we have you we want a cure

So cancer you need to go away
Just die we do pray

Story: Horror Stories

One thing I realized early on after my brother's diagnosis of cancer and this same scenario is common among other cancer patients as well. People want to share stories about cancer.

Why is it that people want to immediately share the horror stories about cancer with the newly diagnosed person and or their families? Do they not think about what a shock it is getting the diagnosis? Do they not think about how scared they are and the high stress level they are already experiencing?

I know in my heart that they are not doing this intentionally. I want to believe that people are just not that insensitive. I do believe they just don't think about what the impact of what they are sharing has on everyone involved.

Sharing stories about fighting, determination, attitude, gratitude, winning and survival are the stories that are appropriate to share. I don't live in a 'Pollyanna' world and neither do those with cancer. We do realize some with cancer will lose the fight, however it does not mean these stories should be shared.

Keep all stories positive, encouraging and uplifting.

Horror Stories ©

By Terry Moore

I have cancer I say,
Soon horror stories rush my way

I don't understand the why
Insensitive people make me want to cry

As if I am not scared enough
Listening to horror stories is really tough

What is gained by the negativity shared
Positive stories are better if you care

The bundle of fearful emotions stirred
Be careful of your stories and your word

Keep it positive keep it sweet
Uplifting stories are best to repeat

So I do have cancer I say
Horror stories I say nah

Waiting ©

By Terry Moore

Waiting is such an ugly game
Learning to be patient is the aim

At the doctor's office we wait
So our time we must donate

We go to the lab for blood draw
We wait again – another flaw

There are multiple procedures and test
Can't say we don't get time to rest

Chemo now that's another story
To heal this is obligatory

Anger we must eliminate
Grateful for having the time to donate

<u>*Just Plain Scared*</u> ©

By Terry Moore

Diagnosed with Cancer
What is the prognosis
I am so scared

I have hopes
I have dreams
I am so unprepared

There are blood draws
Chemo treatments
So many appointments

Feeling shattered
Feeling helpless
Lots of disappointments

What if there's a complication
There is fear
What does my future hold

I have family that I love
I have obligations
It will be ok I've been told

I will learn
I will plan
I will be prepared

Diagnosed with Cancer
Living one day at a time
Learning not to be scared

I am Sick ©

By Terry Moore

I am sick of not feeling right
I am sick of being sick
I am sick of me having to fight

I am sick of not being able to do things
I am sick of the loss of my independence
I am sick of what cancer brings

I am sick of the bruising
I am sick of "How are you feeling"
I am sick of just the losing

I am sick of not having a normal life
I am sick of having to ask for help
I am sick of this cancer causing strife

I am sick of sick, of sick of sick!

Inspirational

Story: Able

When one is diagnosed with cancer it is hard to think about just how able we really are. The mind immediately conjures up all the bad side effects we have heard others talk about. Maybe we should concentrate on all the things we are able to do. We have choices.

We can become bitter or we can stay positive.

We can choose to stay uninformed or we can learn all that we can about this disease.

We can allow ourselves to be depressed or we can say no way.

We can give up or we can fight with all our might.

We can be silent or we can use our voice to get others involved

We can let the disease disable us, or we can work on being who we are

We can keep it all inside or we can cry when we need to and know it's OK

We can be resentful that we need help or we can ask for help and know it's OK

Attitude can make all the difference in the quality of life when dealing with cancer or any other challenging situation that we are faced with. You have to work at being negative and you also have to work to be positive. Choose wisely my friend!

Able ©

By Terry Moore

It's shock-able
It's clock-able

It's why-able
It's cry-able

It's yelp-able
It's help-able

It's clue-able
It's knew-able

It's choose-able
It's do-able

It's fight-able
It's right-able

It's talk-able
It's walk-able

It's grin-able
It's win-able

<u>Cancer you are wrong</u> ©

By Terry Moore

Cancer you are wrong
And wrong you shall be
I won't be intimidated
By the likes of thee

I am my own person
And my own person I shall be
My uniqueness is my own self
My own self I shall be

<u>My Allies</u> ©

By Terry Moore

Cancer you will not win,
I say this with a grin

Nutrition is my ally
So I say to you good bye

Water I will drink a plenty
I will not be low or empty

Rest is a major must
I will do it without fuss

I am in this game to win
I say this with a grin

<u>*Benefits of Cancer*</u> ©

By Terry Moore

Benefits of Cancer there's none,
The worry deletes all fun.

Don't let this be your mindset,
Push it away – please do your best.

Granted there is plenty of stress,
What you want you can manifest.

Attitude of gratitude construct,
Negative attitude deduct.

Negative energy steals,
Use all your energy to heal,

Benefits of Cancer still none,
Stay positive, and remember to have fun.

<u>Between Times</u> ©

By Terry Moore

It's the between time,
It's the 'me' time.

It's slowdown time,
It's get back into the flow time.

It's meditation time,
It's relaxation time.

It's family time,
It's tender time.

It's anything but cancer time,
It's having fun time.

It's giving thanks time,
It's being here on earth time.

Seeking ©

By Terry Moore

I am not seeking answers, but
I seek inspiration

Out of pure desperation

My mission in life is not to thrive; and to just
Merely survive

I want passion, compassion, sprinkled with
Humor and some style

Is this too much to ask for? I think not
Cancer you have met your match

Fairy Tales ©

By Terry Moore

Jack and the bean stalk, and cracker jack box,
Life isn't a fairy tale it does have some hard knocks

Mary had a little lamb and little Bo Peep,
Sometimes things plunge and sometimes things peek

There's Cinderella and Sleeping Beauty and lots of
happy endings,

So keep in mind when life gets tough, there's always
new beginnings

Like hay diddle diddle, the cat and the fiddle and
the cow jumped over the moon

Remember to keep a smile on your face for
your luck can change real soon

For all things we can't control
just remember those old rhymes

Never give up, make your own good luck
And create your own good times

Renew ©

By Terry Moore

Feel like you are at rock bottom now
Ask for help you know how

Pull within and just breathe
Get outdoors and hug a tree

Get grounded, let go, release
Let the tension slowly decrease

The creator knows what you need
There is no reason to plea

Begin to relax and renew
As Mother Nature wraps her arms around you

℘

<u>Pity Party For One</u> ©

By Terry Moore

When things get tough
When I have had enough

When I start building the wall
Because I am too scared to fall

It's time for the 'Pity party for one'
It's my time for fun

It's time to deconstruct the wall
I am strong, I won't fall

Rewriting the end of my story
It's all about survival and glory

A pity party for one is ok
Once in a while, not everyday

I Want It ©

By Terry Moore

I am a survivor
And I won't quit

I have beauty
And I have wit

What I want
I shall get

It's easy for me
Staying focused I won't forget

Determination and hard work
That's all there is to it I swear

Age doesn't matter
So don't even go there

I want it, I will do the work
It's doable I say with a smirk

I am a survivor with no regret
Staying focused I won't forget

My Goal for Life ©

By Terry Moore

My goal for life
To live without strife

See what the universe brings
Seeing the beauty in all things

It might be the beautiful starlight
Or maybe the morning sunlight

It's not about being selective
It's about changing your perspective

It's not about the latest craze
It's about gratitude and praise

Life is a precious gift so live it
Living in harmony is the benefit

My goal for life
Recognize choices for no strife

A life style change ©

By Terry Moore

What's in my future
What will I see

Life style changes
So it must be

Cancer is a disease
I can handle this with ease

Junk food is out
Better choices I now shout

Sugar in moderation
Cuts down on the inflammation

Lots of fresh veggies
No need to get edgy

Lots of water is my friend
Can be infused with a fruity blend

Healthy eating is now in
Taking steps so cancer can't win

Story: Minor Setback

Cancer sometimes seems to be a series of mind games. When you are tired, sick, and feeling just a bit low this is just the opportunity cancer seeks to zap your strength. It is not easy staying positive all the time. In fact it is near impossible but that is ok because we are just human. We have days when we are wore out and want to just hide away and feel sorry for ourselves. It's ok to have these feelings but it is not ok to make it a life style.

The mind knows it is best to stay positive. The mind knows not to give up and not to stop fighting however sometimes it needs a booster shot. Some positive affirmations like "good job", "proud of you", and "don't stop now" may be just the needed strategy. Your body is working overtime trying to beat cancer down so it can't win. The body is amazing and so are you!

Don't let Cancer's minor setbacks destroy you. You have what it takes to beat this. To get a job done takes work so work it! Work at being positive. Work at eating right. Work at being that amazing person you are. Work at beating cancer.

Minor Setback ©

By Terry Moore

A minor setback
It's cancer's mini attack

It's upset that you are strong
Wants to make everything wrong

Don't think of it as a defeat
Fight back; repeat and repeat

You have what it takes
Cancer can't make you break

A minor setback it's a test
You'll win give it your best.

It's not for the weak but the strong
Cancer has no power to make you wrong

Story: All Around Me

By Terry Moore

I am seeing cancer sufferers all around me now, why is that? I think to myself is this like when you buy a new car, let's say a new GMC in a blue color - all of a sudden everywhere you look there is a GMC in blue.

My brother was diagnosed in July and the pop-ups started happening almost immediately. A friend of my brothers was diagnosed with prostate cancer. My brother ran into a female friend of his in a grocery store and she told him she had breast cancer. The lady across the street from me has just been diagnosed with breast cancer. A good friend of mine was just recently was diagnosed with breast, stomach, and bone cancer.

I can't say this isn't making me feel uneasy. I know I am at the age where our bodies are starting to show some wear and tear, but the frosting on the cake should not be cancer.

I have always been grateful for what I have and gratitude journaling is one of my daily practices. I find myself thanking the universe for my good health more often. I find myself being more conscious of taking care of my mind, body and spirit to the best of my ability.

I also have empathy for the ones that are now taking the cancer journey. I make it a point to send little notes of encouragement, love, and compassion. To let them know I care. Letting someone know you are there for them is the best positive energy you can share with them.

<u>All Around Me</u> ©

By Terry Moore

Cancer to the left of me
Cancer to the right

Cancer you are everywhere
You cause such a fright

Do I put blinders on so I don't see
Who's the next one, will it be me

Cancer is all around me now
Stopping this is my vow

I will do what it takes to end this
So we all can live with such bliss

Eradicate cancer to the left of me
Eradicate cancer to the right

Cancer you will be no where
We are ending you causing fright

Story: I am strong

Just read a post from my good friend and I just have to share it with you:

> I will share my journey with you my friends, trying to take
> in what the Dr's have told me, I am strong! I am a fighter,
> and I have an amazing family that supports me. The biopsy
> came back, it is breast cancer and it is in the bone and
> some in the stomach. I am in no pain, it is treatable and
> I am capable of overcoming anything. Love you all, more
> to come.

It saddens me to read this post. My friend is one of the sweetest gals I
have had the pleasure to meet. And once again cancer has struck its nasty
blow. Once again cancer picked someone that is a fighter, a positive thinker,
and amazing artist, and a friend. She will fight and she will win!

I am Strong ©

By Terry Moore

Hear me for I am strong
Cancer you are so wrong

You think I will just give up
You and me are breaking up

You are not a stranger to me
You took the love of my life you see

An amazing family for support I've got
So you see you don't even have a shot

Friends I have plenty
Cancer you don't have any

So be on your way
For here you cannot stay

Story: Cancer Hollywood Style

I was just thinking how Hollywood can make the bleakest circumstances seem easy to correct. It's about the sleight of hand, the wave of a wand, a spell all which gives the seeker just what they want.

Everyone wants to believe in some kind magical solutions for their problems and most refuse to believe in magic. Have you ever took a chance and let yourself believed in magic? Have you ever wished for something and it's magically there for you?

Wouldn't it be wonderful if we could use a sleight of hand, the wave of a magical wand or intentions formed in a spell to get rid of cancer!

On the whimsical side just use your imagination! What if, what if...

<u>A Spell You Say</u> ©

By Terry Moore

Cancer be gone
Wanting this can't be wrong

I have said "I want this" and
"I will do the work"

It's about real Magic
Not Hollywood's quirks

I have put it in writing
I am fully prepared for the fighting

I am strong
So, this is not wrong

So Mote It Be and
Blessed Be

Family Affair

Story: Family Affair

It has been said that cancer is a family affair and anyone who has a loved one with cancer knows this is true. From the impact of the diagnosis, the multiple medical procedures / testing, doctors' appointments, and chemo therapy it turns everyone's world upside down.

At first my brother was numb, and to be honest so was I. Neither one of us was prepared for the diagnosis of cancer. My brother was like a deer in headlights! The look on his face broke my heart.

The first few weeks were really tough on him because he was still in shock. He got appointments confused, couldn't remember steps to complete before test, and he even was in a small fender bender as his thought process was way out of whack due to stress. It was my job to remind him of what was to be completed and when, to be there for him, to reassure him, and to give him support.

As the shock wore off and he was able to settle into his new routine his stress level dropped and he was able to retain details more easily. As he began to function within a lower stress level so did I. A good night's sleep is not over rated for sure.

Family Affair ©

By Terry Moore

Cancer is a family affair,
At the heart strings it does tear.

Everything is turned upside down,
Trying to avoid a meltdown.

The diagnosis horrifies,
Time to neutralize!

Take back the control,
Recognize cancer is a nasty troll.

Cancer is a family affair,
Out of love we will always care.

Cancer and Family Feelings ©

By Terry Moore

When cancer strikes
The whole family has strife

The worry the fears
It creates an overflow of tears

It is the feelings of helplessness
Sleepless nights and restlessness

It hurts to watch them cry
It hurts to watch them wonder why

You want to make it all go away
You are not sure how to behave

You don't want to smother
You don't want to hover

It's the tender touch
It's saying I love you so much

Say you're available and you'll be there
Be understanding and show that you care

<u>Friends</u> ©

By Terry Moore

I just can't do it alone,
I say with a groan.,

It's ok to ask friends,
For needed rest, and to mend.

Some days are like that,
The days you're just a bit off track.

Use your phone,
Need help let it be known.

It's not being bold,
Its ok I've been told.

It's part of self-care
People will help, people do care.

Attitude of Gratitude ©

By Terry Moore

You transport me here and there
I truly appreciate the love that you share

The fact that you care
Makes a difference please be aware

Your patience is beyond measure
You being in my life is a true treasure

You have such a positive attitude
Thank you I say with such gratitude

Love and light
For you being in my life

Story: Let It Out journaling

I signed up for a journaling class called Let It Out. I love to journal so the class name caught my eye but I also knew I needed a place to go that was just for me. I look forward to learning, sharing and bonding with each one in the wonderful class. It is a good fit because when I got home my creative juices where in high gear. Cancer affects the caregiver as much as it affects the cancer patient. Let the healing begin.

Journaling ©

By Terry Moore

The 'Let it out' group is just what I need
Immediately felt at home with Leslie who leads

Introductions from each one there
The group listened and showed that they cared

A cup of coffee and a quiet place to think
My journal in hand and a pen full of ink

Words describing confusion, hurts, and hopes
My safe place to jot down all my souls little notes

I will ponder over times I said yes and should have said no
Writing down my feelings allowing my thoughts to just flow

Clarity and understanding will soon come to me
As the pen glides across the page it is all there for me to see

My journal knows the inner me that I so often hide
Like a good friend it holds my secrets safely tucked inside

<u>Support</u> ©

By Terry Moore

Right now things are a bit grim
He's family and I love him

With all that he is going through
I am sticking by his side like glue

Cancer is taking its toll that's a fact
Affecting us both equals a dual impact

So things won't seem so grim
I am here to support him

We have each other so we are strong
Cancer thinks it will win – it's so wrong

It's my choice I am here to say
I wouldn't have it any other way

Story: Feelings

Cancer stirs up so many emotions. Sometimes I feel nothing at all, it's like I am totally numb. I push the emotions away; I push them deep down inside and try to suppress them because I have to be the strong one. I always have to be the strong one. I am tough, I can handle it. Nothing can hurt me. I won't let it hurt me.

That's a lie!

I feel nothing and I feel everything. I am strong and I am weak. I am learning that everything I am feeling is OK. They are neither right nor wrong. They are just feelings. I will not deny them anymore. I will jot them down and deal with them. I will acknowledge them and feel them.

I am living them and I am feeling them.

<u>Feelings</u> ©

By Terry Moore

I feel sad
I feel lonely
I feel crazy

I feel vulnerable
I feel frustrated
I feel lazy

I feel tired
I feel anger
I feel beat

I feel unhappy
I feel empty
I feel defeat

I feel scared
I feel unsure
I feel used

I feel hurt
I feel stressed
I feel abused

I feel emotional
I feel confused
I feel depressed

I feel nothing
I feel everything
I feel suppressed

Story: Caregiver

The person that helps coordinate care and be there for support is an important person for sure. It is not an easy job to do sometimes. We do it because we care, however we sometimes forget how important it is to take care of ourselves. We put others first and we put ourselves last. Wrong order of doing things! If we don't take care of ourselves then we will not have the energy, patience, and endurance that we need so we can help someone else. It is not selfish to make ourselves first. It is an act of self-love. By giving ourselves self-love we will be capable of providing love, patience, understanding, empathy and support to those we care about.

Care Giver ©

By Terry Moore

We the caregivers GIVE
We want you to live

It has a toll on us
But being strong is a must

We also have a lesson to learn
It's an important concern

Because we care so much
We forget to take care of us

Learning things have to change
Priorities need to be rearranged

By making us first the task is complete
Our body is a temple and ever so sweet

The lesson is right the intention we see
It's important we take care of the ME

By doing so we can continue to give
So we can be there and help you live

Story: Allow

With what I have observed since my brother's diagnosis and watching friends go through the same thing, I have come to realize the same thing is affecting me. Every day we wake up with cancer on our mind.

My brother and I live in different cities however I talk to him every day and I go with him to all his chemo treatments, test and doctor's appointments. Everyday someone is asking me "how is your brother doing. There is NO break when dealing with this disease.

Some days I just want to hang a sign around my neck that says "Please NO cancer talk today". The hardest part of dealing with this disease (disease) is the constant reminders! Some days I just want to scream and other days I want to cry. Other times I am cracking up with light hearted jokes and presenting a whimsical side of dealing with this disease.

Every day I am reminded just how lucky I am to have a brother that is a fighter, a positive thinker, and a doer. He won't let cancer interrupt his daily routine. His uplifting spirit is infectious and it makes it easier to remain positive. On the days he gets a bit down I am in his corner to help him stay positive.

<u>*Allow*</u> ©

By Terry Moore

I've got cancer you say
You think about it everyday

You're allowed to scream
You're allowed to dream

You're allowed to cry
You're allowed to wonder way

You're allowed crackup but
Whatever you do just don't give up

Story: Cancer A Teaching Disease

Cancer is a terrible disease but it is also a teaching disease. As I sit in the chemo clinic with my brother and listen to all the stories shared, it has helped me to learn to stay focused on what is really important to me. We all have problems and there is no way to get around that however, I have learned to spend more time enjoying what I do have and less time worrying about what I don't have. I actually listen to the words spoken as well as the words not spoken. Cancer has taught me to let go of the past, focus on the here and now and not worry so much about the future. I have learned not to take things for granted. I have learned to take the time to tell others how much they mean to me and how grateful I am that they are in my life.

Cancer has taught me the importance of staying positive in a negative situation. Cancer has taught me to reach out for help, to accept help, and to give help.

Did I want this lesson that cancer is giving? No, none of us do but we have a choice of giving up or fighting. We have a choice of learning, to growing, and to be happy. That is one thing cancer can't do and that is having the ability to take away our happiness.

Test And Procedures

Story: MUGA

A multigated acquisition (MUGA) scan creates images of the lower chambers of the heart, the "ventricles". This procedure evaluates if the ventricles are pumping blood properly. It shows any abnormalities in the size of the ventricles and in the movement of the blood through the heart. Some people may need a MUGA scan before chemotherapy to find if there is a pre-existing heart condition.

This was my brother's first test since his diagnosis and boy was he nervous. The fear of the unknown is a major component of his elevated stress levels. After the technician explained the procedure he started to relax just a little bit more. He even started joking with the technician after the injection while we waited for the radioactive material, called a tracer to circulate throughout my brother's body. He tolerated the procedure very well.

<u>MUGA</u> ©

By Terry Moore

MUGA is the first test
My brother is scared I will attest

He's too quiet and that is a sign
He's too proud to whine

I ask the question 'how do you feel'
He smiles and says "it's no big deal"

It's what must be done
I don't expect it to be much fun

I will get through this no doubt
Cancer will not win I want to shout

Story: PET Scan

PET stands for Positron Emission Tomography When PET is used to detect cancer, it allows your doctor to see how the cancer metabolizes, and whether it has spread, or metastasized, to new areas. PET also shows how the tumor is responding to chemotherapy.

My brother is having a problem with this test. To be honest so am I. This test will give us information that we may not be ready to hear but then again we have to know what we are dealing with so we know what lies before us.

My brother is showing signs of overload with this procedure. It is a double edge blade; he wants to know the results and he is too scared to want to know the results. This is his second procedure and he is still in the 'shock stage' of being diagnosed with cancer. His whole life is changing rapidly and it is hard to cope with all the changes that are altering his daily routine. His comfort zone is being disturbed.

<u>*PET scan*</u> ©

By Terry Moore

Oh boy, a PET scan
This procedure I am not a fan

The need to know is there
This is so unfair

My life was good I was not sick
This is such a dirty trick

Nope this is not fair
It's about warfare

Cancer I am ready to fight
I will win this blight

This disease I am not a fan
But willing to fight because I can

Story Bone Marrow Test

The third test scheduled was a bone marrow biopsy and aspiration. This test is done to determine if the cancer has spread to the bone (blood and marrow). They scheduled my brother to have this procedure done in his oncologist office. I think the fact that it was being done by his oncologist instead of strangers helped keep his stress at a lower level. He was still pretty scared and was willing to talk about his concerns.

He was scared of having a small minute incision and the actual procedure for obtaining the bone marrow and aspiration. My 35 years as a nurse in the operating room helped me to be able to explain in layman's terms what was going to happen. I was able to assure him that it wasn't going to be as bad as his mind was building it up to be. We had many conversations about this procedure as new questions popped into his head. I was thankful that I was able remove most of the doubts and fears he had.

It was not so much the procedure that scared him, I think it was the fear of finding out that this disease may have spread to his bone. I was right there with him on this one. I sent out a little prayer to the Universe on this one.

<u>Bone Marrow Biopsy</u> ©

By Terry Moore

Universe hear my request
It's from heart so please do your best

Keep my brother's bone marrow cancer free
So completely whole he can be

Positive I will stay
My conviction will not sway

Cancer free I do pray
By his side I shall stay

Story: First Chemo Day

My brother's first chemo day and boy was he nervous. They accessed the port to infuse the chemo drugs and he stayed quiet. They tried to engage in conversation and he stayed quiet.

He tolerated the treatment really well. He did have a slight headache and a stinging sensation in his nasal cavity but it didn't last long. He experienced no nausea. Eventually he started to joke around with the nurses and he chatted with me as well. He dosed off a few times and I worked on my artwork during this time.

He remained positive throughout the procedure however, he said "I hope to see my 71st birthday". He just turned 70 this month. I smiled and said "you have your bar set too low, so let's shoot for 80+ years. He smiled and said "OK sis, I can do that".

When the treatment was completed he remarked it wasn't as bad as he imagined it would be. He even said if this is all there is to it, it's doable.

I was also relieved that he did not get sick. The hardest part of this whole thing is not having control, and especially not being able to fix it / make it better. I can only shoot to be the best support person that I can be for him and help him handle whatever comes his way. Love will find a way.

Sitting In My Cancer Chair ©

By Terry Moore

Sitting in my chemo chair
All that rhymes I will share:
Infusion & confusion
Fears & Tears
Wiggles & Giggles
Cancer & Answers
Chat & relax
IV & I see
Hair & bare
Snooze & loose
Nurse & converse
Win & grin
Mad & sad
Support & escort
Stress & express
Cried & pride
Drugstore & restore
Me & we
Well & tell

Story: 2ⁿᵈ Chemo

My brother's second chemo session went very well. No side effects to speak of. He had the same stinging in the nasal cavity on the last infusion but again it didn't last long.

The hardest thing for my brother is to listen to the endless chatter from some of the patients. I explained that some patients live alone so when they come to chemo it is their time to socialize. I suggested that he purchase basic ear plugs or to bring his Kindle with ear plugs, then he can listen to the music he likes. He can also read books or play games that will help pass the time away. Having ear plugs will help filter out the room noises so he even has the option to catnap.

Each individual should plan ahead so they are assured to have things they like to do to help pass the time. Chair bound for hours is hard for most people so if one plans ahead the treatment time does not have to be boring.

I take my artwork (sketch book, journal, and watercolors) to keep me busy. I make myself available to chat when my brother feels like chatting but I also allow him to have silent time when he wants it.

I love his attitude!

Passing Time ©

By Terry Moore

In my chemo chair passing time
A TV would be simply divine

The hours slowly pass by
I say this with a slight sigh

Some like to talk
Me, I'd like to walk

Sometimes I read
A good mystery indeed

Sometimes I catnap
Hands folded in my lap

People watching is fun
Studying each one by one

Listening is a skill
Just ask Dr. Phil

Next thing I know – I'm done
I say goodbye to everyone

Story: Whiners

When I sit in the chemo room and I look around at all the beautiful faces and listen to their stories I realize I don't like whiners very much. People that constantly complain about all the little upsets in their life, you know the ones… the "me, me, me kind of people".

Cancer patients don't take things for granted. They are grateful for all the small blessings in their life. Some examples are

- I did not get sick after chemo
- My labs are good so I can get my chemo
- My appetite is good
- I have friends that help
- I am alive
- I am blessed

Lesson learned!

Whiners ©

By Terry Moore

I do not like whiners not one darn bit
If I hear "poor me" one more time I will have a fit

I do not like to hear them in the morning
I do not like them, they are boring

I do not like them in my car
I do not like them near or far

I do not like them in a store
I do not like them on a sea shore

I wish they would go away
I wish here they would not stay

I do not like whiners not one darn bit
I wish they would understand the word 'quit'

Story: Through the Looking Glass

We arrive for the chemo treatment and it's like taking a psychology class. Each chemo patient brings their own way of dealing with having cancer. Some are very quiet and just want to be left alone and get through the treatments as soon as possible. Some get sick with chemo so they lay in the chair very still fighting off the uneasiness they feel inside. Others are really social and love to talk the whole time they are there. They like to swap their chemo stories with others. There are the ones that joke and tease. It helps alleviate the pinned up tension they feel deep down inside.

Many have learned to bring books or electronic devices (tablets and their cell phones) to help pass the time. Chemo treatments are time consuming and distractions make it more bearable. A few manage to sleep through the whole treatment while others take cat naps. Each individual eventually finds what works best for them.

Through the Looking Glass ©

By Terry Moore

Looking through the looking glass
It's like having a psychology class

Each person comes with a tale
This is true for both female and male

Some look like they don't feel well
The whole chemo treatment they repel

Others talk nonstop
Chemo stories they like to swap

Some joke and tease
It's a way for their tension to ease

Some bring books to read
Phones and tablets also fill others needs

Some sleep through the whole thing
A favorite blanket they always bring

The treatments take a chunk of time
Each does their own thing — which is fine

<u>Chemo Nurses</u> ©

By Terry Moore

Chemo nurses what a blessing
Calming effect they are good at manifesting

Compassion and strength they possess
Under pressure they handle the stress

They listen and they care
They chase away any despair

Chemo nurses deserve tons of praise
Their empathy never sways

Chemo nurses as a profession
They are truly a real blessing

Side Effects

Story: Clerk At Drug Store

Months before my brother was diagnosed with cancer I had went into my local drug store and the gal behind the counter ask me how my treatments were going. I was a bit confused and ask why she thought I was sick. She said I had such short hair she presumed that I had cancer. She went on to say that she was diagnosed with cancer and soon would be going through chemo treatments. I wished her well and went on my way.

About 2 months after my initial encounter with the clerk at the drug store I went into that same drug store to pick up some items I needed and ran into her again. She had a hat on so I ask her how her chemo treatments were going. She remarked that she had finished up her treatments and that some of her hair was already growing back now. She took off her hat to show me the new grow and I said "you are stunning with or without hair so strut your stuff". She laughed and said she was trying to get used to going out without a hat on however it still bothered her when people stared at her.

I told her my brother had just been diagnosed with lymphoma and it was also in his bone. I said he would probably lose his hair and when he did I would shave my head in support for what he was about to go through.

She then shared that her mother was just diagnosed with breast cancer. She got huge tears in her eyes and said after having to go through my struggles with this disease now she has to go through the same thing. I wished both her and her mother well in their fight against cancer.

I was so touched by this story that I went home and got one of the cancer inspirational prayer flags that I had made and took it back and gave it to her. I told her that both her and her mother would be in my thoughts and prayers.

The thing that stuck in my mind was the fact that cancer victim's struggle with the disease, treatment and now they have to endure stares because they lost their hair. They wear a wig, hat, or scarves to make others feel more comfortable and also to make themselves feel more whole again.

<u>Still That Same Person</u> ©

By Terry Moore

Don't look at me with eyes filled with pity
I am still that same person; strong and witty

Some side effects I have to endure
As I wait for the cure

Talk to me as you always did
Anything different I forbid

It's a journey some of us have to take
Yes it does create some heartache

I still am that same person; strong and witty
There's no room for self-pity

Story: My Brother Losing His Hair

My brother came to visit today — not his usual day to come but he wanted to show me his hair was coming out by the handfuls. I got out the clippers and ask if he was ready and he said let's do it. It didn't take long and when I started to brush away the cut hair he started to cry. I stopped and sat down by him and just let him cry. I ask what he was feeling and he said I am 70 years old with a good head of hair and this darn disease took it away. He shook his head and said I will be ok; don't know why I am crying.

So, as promised I took the clippers to my head. I am not doing it for attention; I am not doing it for any other reason than to give my brother support. My hair means nothing to me however giving my brother support means everything.

Hair ©

By Terry Moore

One hair, 2 hairs 3 hairs 4,
My hair is falling out on to the flour

Not a problem so that's that,
There are plenty of beautiful hats.

It's about loss of control,
Stay strong I say to console.

You are beautiful no matter what,
Get out there and strut your stuff.

Cancer can't win if,
You can continue to grin.

Story: Side Effects

My brother came to visit today and was explaining that he has had his first bout with chemo side effects. First came the constipation, couldn't go at all. So, he took a laxative to help with the elimination. The bottle said to take two pills and so he did. Then the diarrhea hit hard and fast and his close calls to making it to the bathroom on time began.

After things settled down he began to feel nauseated and was afraid to eat. He was not sure if it was another side effect of the cancer treatment or the pills he took for the constipation. At this point he was afraid to eat for fear that both of these GI upsets would return. I talked him into eating a little something and in a while he began to feel better.

He said he thought it was a small price to pay to keep cancer from having its way and causing more damage. My brother is willing to put up with the discomfort because he wants to win this fight.

<u>Side Effects</u> ©

By Terry Moore

First round of side effects
Two GI upsets

First came – can't go at all
Then whoosh - what a close call

A bit of nausea, not feeling good
Can't eat but know I should

There is medication for this
To be back to normal I wish

I downed the pills
To chase away these ills

It's a small price to pay
So cancer can't have its way

Story: Additional Side Effects

∽

My brother informed me that he is experiencing more symptoms from the change in his chemo treatments. He is feeling the blahs, not sick but not feeling well either. Another change is he has lost the ability to taste his food. He knew it might happen, he does not like that it is happening however he knows it is what it is and he will have to deal with it.

He seemed to be a bit down today and I suggested that he get out and visit some of his good friends. When a person sits in the house and dwells on the negative side effects it can really lead to depression.

I can help him work through the issues and make suggestions to help him change how he reacts to the situation. I validate all his feeling and I also show him empathy in what he is going through. My job is to help him get out of his funky mood.

He is heading out to visit his friends and I will call him tonight to check on him. One thing that I admire about my brother; he refuses to let cancer get the better of him. He knows he can come to me to talk about anything and everything. He is open to suggestions and he wants to stay positive.

I have an awesome brother.

ß

<u>Inconvenient</u> ©

By Terry Moore

I am feeling a little under the weather
My white count is lower than ever

Some precautions need to be met
So viruses and infections can't be a threat

If you are sick please stay away
Bend the rules I say nay

Wearing a mask is a must
Please don't make such a fuss

It's inconvenient for both you and me
It's a needed precaution can't you see

It won't be forever please understand
I am fighting cancer so I am taking a stand

Changes ©

By Terry Moore

My taste buds are gone
This is just so wrong

I like my food to taste good
Food should taste normal, I wish it would

I have the blahs, just not feeling right
My immune system is giving a good fight

I acknowledge I am a bit down
I say this with a slight frown

My attitude needs a touch up
I am strong so I refuse to give up

It's a small setback and I'll be okay
I will manage it day by day

Story: Side effect; Blood Clot

My brother showed up at my home around 10:30 am worried about the size of his arm. He woke up with an aching sensation in his arm pit and his arm was twice its size. So, off to the emergency room we go to find out what is happening.

After the initial examination and knowing he had a med port for cancer treatments he was sent to vascular lab for a Doppler Ultrasound. It didn't take them long to see a good size clot that was causing the problem. Next stop was to an have x-ray to check out his lungs and surround area.

He was given a bolus of Heparin (a blood thinner) and was admitted for observation. He will spend a couple of days in the hospital to make sure the prescribed treatment is working.

This rattled my brother pretty good. He was scared of the clot moving and possibly having a stroke or even death. It took a lot of reassuring from the medical staff and me to convince him that he would be ok.

After he got settled into his private room he became much more relaxed. We talked a bit on what the doctors had just told him. It is just a small set back and a real inconvenience however Cancer is not winning this fight. My brother is not going to let this dampen his spirits – he is a fighter.

<u>Tormentor</u> ©

By Terry Moore

Woke up, something is not right
My arm is swollen and tight

Off to the emergency room I go
I have a real need to know

Scheduled for a vascular ultrasound
A blood clot they quickly found

Next was x-ray to check out my lungs
I am having so much fun

Another setback cancer has sent
Meds prescribed to help prevent

Now it is blood thinning time
Over time I will be fine

Cancer come front and center
You will not be my tormentor

Story: Blood Thinners

My brother formed a blood clot that originated from the site of the med port. Now he has to be on blood thinners for at least the next 3 months. He is a typical man and usually doesn't think about what he is doing when is fixing things because his focus is getting the job done. It almost seems that he develops a new bruise every day.

I was joking with him and sad he looked as if he got in a fight. People are always asking him "what happened to you". When they find out he is on blood thinners that cause the bruising he then hears "I hope you improve soon". He tells me his new color is black and blue.

We try to find some kind of humor in the whole ordeal of fighting against cancer. It is easier to make light of the situation than it is to be all sad and mad that one has to be in this situation.

Blood Thinners ©

By Terry Moore

Blood thinners what a mess
I bruise so easy I attest

It looks like I've been in a fight
I have to admit I am quite a sight

The questions "what happened to you"
And "oh my I hope you soon improve"

Cancer has created this plight
It's part of the cure to make me right

Black and blue is my color now
What a production, I take a bow

Victory

<u>Many Victories</u> ©

By Terry Moore

Victories are everywhere
You just have to be aware

You wake up to sunshine
You listen to wind chimes

It's the smile from another
For me it's from my brother

It is the energy to shop
It is the energy to mop

A good friend calls to say hello
You enjoy a good TV show

Nothings better than good eats
Morning coffee can't be beat

It's having no pain
It's listening to the rain

It's the large and the small
It's enjoying it all

<u>Ribbon of Victory</u> ©

By Terry Moore

Cancer you reared your ugly head
That is why we have cancer meds

The pain and the suffering
We have support for buffering

The havoc you cause
I am so appalled

You think you are winning, you're not
In fact you don't even have a shot

We are determined and we are strong
Out to prove that you are wrong

It's a war that we have declared
The ribbon of victory we shall wear

Story: End of R-Chop

I was so excited when it came to the end of the R-chop treatment. My brother went through all 9 cycles without any side effects except for the loss of taste a few times and constipation that was relieved by daily supplements.

Another CT scan was scheduled after his final chemo treatment and during his post scan visit his oncologist said the mass by his kidneys had not decreased as much as she would have liked. Her recommendation was to send him to a larger institution that specializes in cancer for their opinion.

After seeing a new set of specialist that evaluated the mass near the kidney my brother was told it was not cancer and that it was scar tissue. They will continue to monitor him. They said he is done with chemo and he will not need to be scheduled for chemo a maintenance program so his med port can be removed.

This was great news for my brother and I am so thankful for the positive outcome.

Predictions ©

By Terry Moore

The R-Chop treatment is at an end
This is what they recommend

Symptoms is the <u>determinant</u>
The bone marrow cancer is permanent

The waiting and the unknowing
Clues for the end are now showing

Keeping it positive keeping it sweet
This cancer can still be beat

Not a coward not a fool
Cancer I challenge you to a duel

Not giving up for I am strong
Going to prove this prediction is wrong

Story: My Way / End of Life Request

I have a good friend who's daughter gave a tremendous fight against cancer however nothing was working so the next step was hospice. This courageous young woman decided things were going to be done her way. She wanted her remaining time to be a celebration of life not the downside of pending death.

She wanted decorations, theme parties, balloons, cake, cupcakes, funny little talks about whimsical light-hearted things. No doom or gloom allowed. She stayed upbeat and happy until the end. She won the fight in her own way as she never allowed cancer to take away her happiness.

<u>My Way</u> ©

By Terry Moore

What I want I will say
I want things done my way

I want a party so let us get hats
Let's have lots of silly chitchats

A cup cake with a candle
Lots of frosting I can handle

I want to celebrate life
Getting away from cancer strife

Cancer you can't take away my joy
It's my life – I won't let you annoy

Let it be whimsical and fun
It's my way until I am done

Story: Last CT Scan and Scheduled Maintenance.

On November my brother had another CT scan as a follow up to the previous one. The report stated the nodules in my brother's lungs are not cancer but scar tissue. His lab work is all normal so the conclusion is he is lymphoma free. He still has bone marrow cancer so for three years he will see his oncologist every 3 months and for another two years after that he will see his oncologist every 6 months. If all is clear after the total of five years he will not have to see an oncologist. He will continue to see his primary physician for blood work to monitor his bone marrow cancer. He has no issues with it and hopefully will not have any in the future.

My brother has remained positive through this whole ordeal. He has made up his mind that he will continue the fight by eating right, he joined a gym to keep his weight down. He continues to drink plenty of water and he has a daily routine. He is an amazing, positive, lover of life. He plans on enjoying each day and his number one rule is to be happy!

CPSIA information can be obtained
at www.ICGtesting.com
Printed in the USA
FFOW03n0941010218
44816239-44950FF

9 781543 480795